ANNE FRANK FOR KIDS

THE LIFE AND TIMES OF ANNE FRANK

VIRGINIA GRANT

BOOKSTEM

Copyright © 2025 by Virginia Grant

All rights reserved.

No part of this book may be reproduced in any form or by any electronic or mechanical means, including information storage and retrieval systems, without written permission from the author, except for the use of brief quotations in a book review.

CONTENTS

Introduction   5

1. A GIRL NAMED ANNE   9
   Her family   11
   What Anne loved to do as a child   15
   The growing tensions in Germany   18

2. LIFE IN AMSTERDAM   23
   School, friends   26
   The rise of Adolf Hitler   28
   How life started changing for Jewish
   people in the Netherlands   31

3. HIDING IN THE SECRET ANNEX   35
   Anti-Jewish laws   39
   Otto Frank's plan to hide to keep his
   family safe   42
   Moving into the Secret Annex   46
   What life was like in hiding   49

4. ANNE'S DIARY   53
   How her diary became her best friend   56
   What Anne wrote about   58
   The hardships of hiding   60

5. DISCOVERY AND CAPTURE   63
   The betrayal   65
   Anne and her family being arrested   67

6. THE JOURNEY TO THE CAMPS 69
   Life in the concentration camps 71
   Anne and Margot being sent to
   Bergen-Belsen 74

7. ANNE'S LEGACY 79
   How Anne's words were published 81
   How Anne's diary has inspired
   millions of people around the world 84

Conclusion 89
Appendix 93

INTRODUCTION

Anne Frank was a real girl who lived during a time when the world was in great danger. She wasn't a queen, a scientist, or a famous leader. She was a regular girl who had dreams, worries, and favorite things, just like any other child. But something set her apart—her words.

She wrote in a diary, not knowing that her words would travel across the world, be read by millions, and help people understand what life was like for Jewish families during World War II. She didn't plan to become famous. She just wrote what she felt, and because of that, we know her story today.

People often think of history as something that only belongs to textbooks, filled with dates and facts about events that happened long ago. But history is made up of real people—people who laughed, cried, and had hopes for the future. Anne Frank is one of those people. Her diary gives us a glimpse into what it was like to live in hiding during a time when the world was very dangerous for Jewish families.

Most stories about the past are written by adults looking back at what happened. But Anne's diary is different. She wrote it while everything was happening around her. She didn't know what the future held. She didn't know what would happen to her family or how long they would have to stay hidden. That makes her story even more powerful. It's not someone looking back with all the answers— it's the voice of a young girl living through the unknown, writing about her fears, frustrations, and dreams as they happened.

Anne was born in 1929, in Germany, at a time when things were starting to change. People were struggling with money, and new leaders were coming into power. One of those leaders, Adolf Hitler, blamed Jewish people for problems they had nothing to do with. He spread lies and made rules that took away the rights of Jewish families, including Anne's. Her parents made the difficult decision to leave Germany and move to the Netherlands, hoping they would be safer there.

For a while, life in Amsterdam was peaceful. Anne made friends, went to school, and enjoyed her favorite books. But then the war reached the Netherlands, and everything changed again. New rules took away her freedom. She wasn't allowed to go to certain places, her father had to give up his business, and Jewish people were no longer treated as equals. Eventually, it became clear that her family was in danger, and they had no choice but to hide.

This is where Anne's diary becomes so important. It shows what life was like when her family went into hiding in a secret apartment, known as the Secret Annex. For more than two years, she wrote about her life—what she thought, what she hoped for, and how she felt about the world. She didn't just write about the war. She wrote about missing fresh air, about arguments with the other people in hiding, about feeling trapped, and about growing up in a space where there was no privacy.

Anne was honest. She didn't try to make herself sound perfect. She wrote about her emotions, whether she was feeling hopeful or frustrated. She questioned the world around her and thought about big ideas—about people, about fairness, and about what she wanted her life to be like when the war was over.

One of the most powerful things about her diary is that it reminds people that history isn't just about leaders and battles. It's about families, friendships, and the choices people had to make to survive. When people read Anne's words, they don't just learn about what happened during World War II. They connect with her as a person, as if she's speaking directly to them across time.

Her diary was never meant to be famous. She started writing for herself, but as time went on, she began hoping that one day, her words would be published. She wanted people to know what it was like to live in hiding. She wanted to share her thoughts with the world.

After the war, Anne's father, Otto Frank, found her diary and made the difficult decision to share it with others. It was heartbreaking for him to read her words, but he knew they were important. When her diary was published, it changed the way people understood what happened during the Holocaust. It wasn't just numbers and statistics anymore—it was a real girl's experience.

1

A GIRL NAMED ANNE

Anne Frank was born on June 12, 1929, in the city of Frankfurt, Germany. She was the second daughter of Otto and Edith Frank. Her sister, Margot, was three years older. The Frank family was Jewish, but they weren't very religious. They celebrated holidays like Hanukkah, but they also lived a modern life. They had a nice home, enjoyed books and music, and spent time with friends and neighbors from different backgrounds.

Frankfurt was a busy city with tall buildings, crowded streets, and markets filled with people selling food and goods. Anne's family lived in a comfortable apartment, and she had a happy childhood in her early years. She played outside, went to the park, and enjoyed spending time with her sister. Margot was quiet and serious, but Anne was full of energy and loved to talk. She was curious about everything, always asking questions and sharing her thoughts.

Anne liked attention and often made people laugh. She wasn't shy, and she had a way of making friends quickly. Even as a small child, she had strong opinions and wasn't afraid to speak her mind. Her father, Otto, encouraged her curiosity. He read to her and helped her find answers to her many questions. He believed that learning was one of the most important things a person could do. Anne admired him and loved spending time with him.

Her mother, Edith, was quieter and more reserved. She took care of the household and made sure her daughters were well-behaved. Anne sometimes felt closer to her father than to her mother, which she later wrote about in her diary. She wanted to be understood, and she didn't always feel that way at home.

Life in Frankfurt was good for the Franks, but things were changing in Germany. In the early 1930s, a man named Adolf Hitler became the leader of the country. He was the head of a political group called the Nazis. The Nazis believed that some people were better than others, and they blamed Jewish people for problems in Germany. They spread lies, saying that Jewish families were the reason the country was struggling.

Otto and Edith Frank saw what was happening. Jewish businesses were being boycotted, meaning people were told not to shop at stores owned by Jewish families. Newspapers printed hateful messages, and Jewish people were starting to lose their rights.

At first, Anne was too young to understand the changes. She was more focused on playing with her dolls, listening to stories, and spending time with her friends. But as time went on, life became more difficult for Jewish families in Germany. Some people stopped talking to them. Jewish children were no longer welcome in certain schools. People who had once been neighbors and friends started treating them differently.

Her family

Anne Frank grew up in a family that cared deeply for one another. Her parents, Otto and Edith Frank, worked hard to give their two daughters, Margot and Anne, a happy and secure childhood. They valued education, kindness, and family, and these beliefs shaped the way Anne saw the world.

OTTO FRANK WAS THOUGHTFUL, intelligent, and patient. He had been a soldier in World War I and came from a family that had been successful in business. After the war, he worked in banking and later took over a company that sold pectin, an ingredient used in making jam. He loved to read and encouraged his daughters to do the same. He believed that learning was one of the most important things a person could do, and he made sure Anne and Margot had access to books, lessons, and discussions that would help them grow.

OTTO HAD a calm way of dealing with problems. He didn't get angry easily, and he didn't raise his voice often. Anne felt close to him because he listened to her and took her thoughts seriously. Even when she was small, he encouraged her to ask questions and express her opinions. She later wrote in her diary that she saw him as her favorite parent. She felt understood by him in a way she didn't always feel with her mother.

. . .

EDITH FRANK WAS QUIETER and more traditional in how she raised her children. She focused on making sure her daughters were polite, well-behaved, and responsible. She was devoted to her family and worked hard to create a peaceful home, even when the world outside was becoming more dangerous. Anne sometimes felt that Edith didn't understand her as well as Otto did. She thought her mother favored Margot, who was more obedient and serious, while Anne was more outspoken and energetic.

EDITH WORRIED A LOT, especially as the situation in Germany got worse. She saw how Jewish families were being treated unfairly, and she wanted to protect her daughters from what was happening. When the family moved to the Netherlands, she had a hard time adjusting. She missed Germany and the life they had left behind. Even in Amsterdam, when things seemed better, she stayed on guard, afraid that danger would follow them.

. . .

MARGOT FRANK WAS the older sister. She was three years older than Anne and very different in personality. While Anne was lively and talkative, Margot was quiet, studious, and well-behaved. She excelled in school and followed the rules without question. People often described her as polite, kind, and responsible.

BECAUSE MARGOT WAS SO WELL-MANNERED, adults often compared Anne to her, which annoyed Anne. She didn't want to be like Margot. She wanted to be herself—someone who asked questions, spoke her mind, and didn't always follow the rules. Margot and Anne cared about each other, but they weren't very close. They had different interests, different ways of looking at the world, and different relationships with their parents.

EVEN THOUGH THEY WERE DIFFERENT, there were moments when Anne admired Margot. She was intelligent, hardworking, and thoughtful. But she also seemed distant at times, as if she were already an adult while Anne was still trying to figure things out. Margot didn't get into trouble, didn't argue much, and didn't challenge their parents the way Anne did.

THE FRANK FAMILY had a strong bond, even when there were disagreements. They supported one another through difficult times and made decisions together when the world around them became dangerous. Each person played a different role—Otto as the steady leader, Edith as the protective mother, Margot as the responsible older sister, and Anne as the curious and energetic younger daughter. Their relationships weren't perfect, but they stayed together and tried to create a sense of normalcy even when life became unpredictable.

What Anne loved to do as a child

Anne Frank was full of energy. She was the kind of child who never liked to sit still for too long. She had a quick mind, a loud laugh, and a way of making people notice her wherever she went. She was curious about everything and always had something to say. She loved asking questions, sharing her thoughts, and making up stories.

Books were one of her greatest joys. She loved to

read, and once she found a book she liked, she wouldn't put it down until she had finished every page. She read fairy tales, adventure stories, and books about history. She liked exciting stories, especially ones about strong, brave characters who went on great journeys. Unlike some children who needed to be told to read, Anne needed to be reminded to take breaks from reading. She could spend hours lost in a book, turning the pages as fast as she could.

Writing was just as important to her. She didn't just enjoy reading stories—she wanted to create them. She wrote down her thoughts, observations, and ideas. She wrote letters, short stories, and descriptions of things she found interesting. She liked making lists of her favorite things and writing about her dreams for the future. Long before she kept her famous diary, she was already writing about the world as she saw it.

She wasn't the kind of child who kept all her thoughts to herself. She wanted to share them. If she had an idea, she spoke up. If she found something funny, she laughed loudly. If she disagreed with something, she wasn't afraid to say so. She was full of opinions and wasn't shy about sharing them. This made her stand out, especially in her family.

Anne also loved to be around people. She had a lot of friends and was always looking for someone to talk to or play with. She enjoyed games, telling jokes, and making people laugh. She could be playful and mischievous, sometimes teasing her friends or challenging them in silly competitions. She was confident and bold, never afraid to be herself.

Even though she loved being around others, she didn't always get along with everyone. Her strong personality sometimes led to arguments, especially at home. She could be impatient, and when she felt frustrated, she let people know. She didn't like being told what to do, and she didn't always follow rules the way her older sister, Margot, did. While Margot was quiet and obedient, Anne was full of questions and opinions.

School was another place where Anne's personality showed. She was smart, but she didn't always focus on her lessons the way her teachers wanted her to. She was talkative and sometimes got in trouble for speaking out of turn. Teachers liked her intelligence but sometimes found her a little too energetic. Even when she was told to be quiet, she found ways to whisper to her friends or pass notes.

She had a love for adventure. Whether it was exploring outside, coming up with stories, or making up games, she was always looking for something fun to do. She wasn't someone who liked to sit back and watch—she wanted to be in the middle of the action. If there was a group of kids playing, she joined in. If there was a new game to try, she wanted to be the first to test it out.

The growing tensions in Germany

By the early 1930s, life in Germany was starting to change in ways that made Jewish families, including the Franks, uneasy. Anne was too young to understand what was happening, but the adults around her could see the signs of trouble. Otto and Edith Frank had built a good life in Frankfurt, but the country they called home was becoming more dangerous for Jewish people.

Germany had been struggling since the end of World War I. Many people had lost their jobs, businesses were failing, and prices for food and other goods were rising quickly. Families who had once been comfortable found themselves struggling to afford basic necessities. People were frustrated and angry, and some were looking for someone to blame.

That was when Adolf Hitler and his political group, the Nazis, began to gain power. They spread the idea that Germany's problems were caused by certain groups of people, especially Jewish families. This wasn't true, but the Nazis used speeches, newspapers, and posters to convince people that Jewish citizens were to blame. Slowly, these false ideas started to spread, and more people began to believe them.

Hitler became the leader of Germany in 1933. Almost immediately, he and the Nazis started passing laws that targeted Jewish people. Jewish businesses were boycotted, which meant that people were told not to shop at them. Jewish workers, teachers, and lawyers lost their jobs. New rules made life more difficult, and Jewish families started feeling unwelcome in their own neighborhoods.

Anne's parents saw these changes happening and worried about what it would mean for their family. Otto had fought for Germany in World War I, and he loved his country, but he could see that things were becoming dangerous. He and Edith had hoped that life would return to normal, but instead, things only got worse.

People who had been their neighbors and customers for years started acting differently. Some stopped speaking to Jewish families, afraid they would get in trouble if they were seen being friendly.

Others openly supported the Nazis, repeating the lies they had heard about Jewish people. The Franks were not the only ones experiencing this. Many Jewish families across Germany were realizing that they might not be safe in their own country anymore.

Then came the biggest change of all—Jewish children were no longer allowed to attend the same schools as non-Jewish children. That meant Margot, Anne's older sister, would have to leave her school and go to a separate one just because she was Jewish. It was another way the Nazis were trying to push Jewish people out of German society.

Otto knew that things were only going to get worse. He made the difficult decision to leave Germany and start over in another country. He chose the Netherlands, hoping that his family could find safety there. The Netherlands had not been affected by Nazi rule, and it seemed like a place where Jewish families could live without fear.

In 1933, Otto left first to set up a new life in Amsterdam. He found an apartment and started a business selling pectin, an ingredient used to make jam. A few months later, Edith, Margot, and four-year-old Anne followed him to their new home.

Anne was too young to fully understand why

they were moving. To her, it felt like an adventure. She had to say goodbye to the only home she had ever known, but she was excited about living in a new place. She didn't know that her parents had left because they had no choice. If they had stayed in Germany, they would have been in danger.

2

LIFE IN AMSTERDAM

Moving to Amsterdam was a big change for Anne Frank and her family. They had left behind everything they knew in Germany—their home, their friends, and their extended family. But for Anne, who was only four years old when they arrived, Amsterdam quickly became her new world. She was young enough to adapt easily, and she threw herself into life in her new city.

Amsterdam was different from Frankfurt in many ways. The streets were lined with tall, narrow houses that leaned slightly forward over the canals. Bicycles were everywhere, and boats moved through the waterways like cars did in other cities. People spoke Dutch instead of German, and while Otto and

Edith had to work to learn the language, Anne and Margot picked it up quickly.

Margot started school first, and as always, she was a good student. She worked hard and followed the rules. When it was time for Anne to begin school, she was eager to go. She had always been full of energy and curiosity, and she was excited to meet new people. She made friends easily and was always chatting with her classmates. She was the kind of child who stood out—she was quick to speak up, full of ideas, and not afraid to express her opinions.

She was also a little mischievous. While Margot was known for being quiet and responsible, Anne had a harder time sitting still. Teachers noticed that she liked to talk more than she liked to listen, and she sometimes got in trouble for interrupting. She was bright, and she did well in school when she focused, but she was much more interested in playing, reading stories, and spending time with friends.

One of Anne's favorite places in Amsterdam was Merwedeplein, the square where her family lived. The Frank family's apartment was comfortable, and from their windows, they could see children playing outside. Anne spent hours running around with her friends, playing games, and coming up with little adventures. She was always surrounded by people, laughing and talking, always eager to be part of the fun.

At home, she was just as lively. She and Margot had different personalities, which sometimes led to small arguments, but they cared about each other. Anne admired Margot's intelligence, even if she didn't always want to be like her. She wanted to be noticed in her own way. She was confident, opinionated, and determined to make her mark.

Otto, as always, encouraged Anne's curiosity. He brought home books, read to her, and answered her endless questions. He understood her better than anyone and always made time to listen. Edith, on the other hand, sometimes found Anne's energy exhausting. She was used to Margot's quiet, obedient nature, and Anne's strong personality could be difficult to manage.

Even though Amsterdam felt like home, the Franks never forgot why they had left Germany. Otto kept a close eye on what was happening there. He saw that the Nazis were passing more and more laws that made life harder for Jewish people. Even though they were safe in the Netherlands, he knew things could change.

School, friends

Anne Frank loved being around people, and that made school one of her favorite places. She wasn't the kind of student who always sat quietly and followed every rule, but she was clever, curious, and full of energy. Her teachers noticed her quick mind, but they also noticed how much she liked to talk. If there was a conversation happening, Anne wanted to be part of it. If there was a joke being told, she wanted to be the one making people laugh.

She was bright enough to do well in her lessons, but she didn't always focus the way her teachers wanted her to. She could be playful and a little stubborn, especially when she was supposed to be paying attention. Sometimes, she had to be reminded to stop talking and finish her work. She was full of ideas, and she liked to share them, even if it wasn't the right time.

Despite her tendency to get distracted, Anne enjoyed learning. She liked reading, especially books that had adventure and excitement. She had a strong imagination and loved stories that took her to different places. She also enjoyed history and languages, though she wasn't as fond of math.

Outside of school, she had plenty of friends. She

was outgoing and made friends easily, always looking for someone to talk to or play with. She wasn't shy about introducing herself and was quick to turn a stranger into a friend. She had a large circle of people she spent time with, and she loved being surrounded by others.

One of her best friends was Hanneli Goslar, who had also moved to the Netherlands from Germany. They spent a lot of time together, talking about school, books, and whatever was on their minds. They walked to school together, played outside, and visited each other's homes. Anne also had other close friends, including Jacqueline van Maarsen. Each friend was different, but Anne found ways to connect with all of them.

She liked to be the center of attention, whether she was playing games, telling stories, or making people laugh. She could be a little dramatic at times, especially when she wanted to prove a point. If she was frustrated, she let people know. If she was excited, she was bursting with energy.

Her days were filled with simple joys—playing outside, roller-skating, riding her bike, and going to the movies. She loved films and admired actresses, often daydreaming about what it would be like to be famous. She wrote about this in her diary years later, imagining herself as a writer or someone important. She wanted to do something big with her life, though she wasn't sure what it would be yet.

At home, things were sometimes less fun. She and her older sister, Margot, had different personalities, and that sometimes led to small arguments. Margot was more obedient, quiet, and focused on school, while Anne was full of opinions and liked to challenge things. Their mother, Edith, often tried to get Anne to behave more like Margot, which frustrated Anne.

The rise of Adolf Hitler

While Anne was enjoying her childhood in Amsterdam, events in Europe were moving in a dangerous direction. Adolf Hitler had become the leader of Germany in 1933, and under his rule, life for Jewish families was becoming more difficult. The Frank family had already left Germany to escape the new laws that targeted Jewish people, but Hitler's influence wasn't stopping at Germany's borders. It was spreading into other countries, bringing fear and uncertainty with it.

Hitler and his Nazi party believed in an idea that some people were more important than others. They blamed Jewish people, as well as other groups, for Germany's problems, even though they had done nothing wrong. The Nazis used newspapers, radio broadcasts, and speeches to spread their beliefs. They convinced many Germans to turn against their Jewish neighbors, teachers, and shop owners. Jewish businesses were taken away, Jewish children were removed from schools, and families were forced to leave their homes.

At first, these changes were happening in Germany. But Hitler had bigger plans. He wanted Germany to be the most powerful country in Europe, and he was willing to use force to make it happen. He began building up his military and taking control of land outside of Germany. In 1938, German troops marched into Austria, claiming it as part of Germany. A few months later, they took over part of Czechoslovakia. Other countries, including the Netherlands, watched nervously as Hitler gained more power.

For a while, many people hoped that war could be avoided. Some leaders in Europe thought that if they let Hitler take a little land, he would stop. But he didn't stop. In September 1939, German soldiers invaded Poland. This time, other countries, including Britain and France, had no choice but to respond. World War II had begun.

At first, the Netherlands was not part of the war. The Dutch government wanted to stay neutral, just as they had in World War I. Many people in Amsterdam hoped that their country would be left alone, that they could continue their lives without being dragged into the growing conflict. But in May 1940, those hopes were shattered. German forces invaded the Netherlands.

The attack was swift and brutal. The Dutch army fought back, but they were not strong enough to stop the German military. After just a few days, the situation became even worse. German planes bombed the city of Rotterdam, destroying large parts of it. The Dutch government, knowing they could not win, surrendered. The Netherlands was now under Nazi control.

At first, life in Amsterdam didn't change overnight. Stores remained open, people still went to school, and families tried to continue as they always had. But things were different. German soldiers were in the streets, and new rules were being introduced. Many people feared what would happen next.

How life started changing for Jewish people in the Netherlands

At first, life in Amsterdam didn't change much after the Nazis took control. People still went to work, children still went to school, and businesses remained open. But underneath the surface, things were beginning to shift. The German soldiers were everywhere, and the Dutch government was no longer in charge. The Nazis were making the rules now, and they had very clear ideas about how they wanted things to be.

JEWISH FAMILIES, like the Franks, paid close attention to these changes. They had already experienced what it was like to be treated unfairly in Germany, and they knew what the Nazis were capable of. At first, the new rules were small, things that didn't seem to affect daily life too much. Jewish people had to register with the government, listing their names and addresses. It seemed like just paperwork, but it was the beginning of something much more serious.

. . .

THEN, new restrictions started appearing. Jewish people couldn't work in certain jobs anymore. Doctors, teachers, and business owners lost their positions. Some families were forced to sell their businesses or hand them over to non-Jewish workers. Jewish children were told they could no longer attend the same schools as other Dutch children.

FOR ANNE, this meant saying goodbye to the school she had loved and moving to a separate school for Jewish students. She was lucky to still be able to learn, but it didn't feel the same. Her world, which had once been filled with different friends and opportunities, was growing smaller.

EACH NEW RULE made life a little harder. Jewish people weren't allowed in certain public places—parks, movie theaters, libraries, and even swimming pools. Signs appeared in shop windows saying that Jewish customers were no longer welcome. Families who had once felt safe in Amsterdam were beginning to feel like outsiders in their own city.

. . .

ONE OF THE biggest changes was the yellow star. The Nazis required all Jewish people to wear a yellow Star of David on their clothing, making them easy to identify. This meant that even in a crowd, it was obvious who was Jewish and who wasn't. People who had once been friendly started treating their Jewish neighbors differently. Some looked away, pretending not to see them. Others crossed the street to avoid them. There were still people who were kind and tried to help, but fear kept many silent.

OTTO FRANK UNDERSTOOD that these rules were leading to something worse. He had seen it happen in Germany, and he knew it was only a matter of time before Jewish families would be in even greater danger. Some families had already started disappearing—taken from their homes by Nazi officers and sent to unknown places. Rumors spread about what was happening, but no one knew the full truth yet.

3

HIDING IN THE SECRET ANNEX

On May 10, 1940, the German army invaded the Netherlands. The Dutch military tried to defend their country, but the German forces were too strong. Within days, the skies over the Netherlands were filled with Nazi warplanes, and German troops moved quickly through the streets. The people of Amsterdam had hoped their country would remain neutral, as it had during World War I, but now it was clear that there was no escape from war this time.

At first, many Dutch citizens believed that life might go on as usual under German rule. Shops and schools remained open, and families tried to carry on with their daily routines. But Jewish families, including the Franks, understood that things would only get worse. They had already seen what happened to Jewish people in Germany. They had seen rights taken away, businesses shut down, and neighbors forced out of their homes. Now, those same things were beginning to happen in the Netherlands.

Within months of the invasion, the Nazis started passing new laws against Jewish people. These rules were designed to separate them from the rest of society and make life increasingly difficult. Jewish businesses were taken over by non-Jewish owners, Jewish children had to attend separate schools, and public spaces were closed to them. The yellow Star of David had to be worn at all times. Every new rule was a reminder that Jewish people were no longer welcome in their own country.

The Franks had been watching these changes carefully. Otto Frank, always thoughtful and cautious, had already begun preparing for the worst. He had seen too much in Germany to believe that things would simply get better on their own. He started making arrangements for a possible hiding place—somewhere his family could go if things became too dangerous. He spoke to a few trusted employees from his business and slowly put together a plan.

By 1942, the situation had grown even more dangerous. The Nazis had started arresting Jewish people and deporting them to unknown locations. People would be taken from their homes, put onto trucks or trains, and never seen again. No one knew exactly where they were being sent, but there were rumors that these people were not just being moved to other cities—they were being sent to camps, and they weren't coming back.

The Frank family knew they had to disappear before it was too late. On July 5, 1942, Margot Frank received a letter ordering her to report for work duty. This was not a choice. Jewish people who were given these orders had to obey, or they would be taken by force. Otto and Edith Frank did not wait to find out what would happen if Margot went. They knew it was time to leave their home and go into hiding.

The plan had been in place for a while, but now it had to happen immediately. The Franks packed only the things they could carry. They wore as many layers of clothing as possible so they wouldn't have to bring suitcases that would make them look suspicious. They left behind their furniture, their dishes, and everything that made their apartment feel like home. Anne even had to leave behind her beloved cat.

Their hiding place was the Secret Annex, a concealed section of Otto Frank's business building. It was located behind a bookshelf that had been specially designed to hide the entrance. From the outside, it looked like just another part of the building, but behind the hidden door was a space where eight people would soon be living in complete secrecy.

Moving into the Annex meant leaving behind everything they knew. It meant no more fresh air, no more playing outside, no more trips to school or visits with friends. It meant living in silence during the day so that no one in the office below would hear them. It meant being completely dependent on the kindness of a few trusted helpers who would bring them food, supplies, and news from the outside world.

The transition was difficult. The Secret Annex was small, and with eight people living together, privacy barely existed. Anne, always full of energy and curiosity, struggled with the new restrictions. She was used to speaking her mind and moving freely. Now, she had to whisper, stay inside, and live by strict rules. The change was frustrating for everyone, but they all understood that there was no other option.

While the world outside continued to change, the people inside the Secret Annex did their best to create a sense of normal life. Otto Frank kept the children focused on their studies, making sure they continued to read and write. They all found ways to pass the time—Margot studied, Edith tried to keep things organized, and Anne turned to her diary. Writing became her way of making sense of everything that was happening.

Anti-Jewish laws

Before the Franks went into hiding, life for Jewish families in the Netherlands had become almost unbearable. One law after another was put in place, each one designed to take away their rights and isolate them from the rest of society. These weren't just rules about where they could go or what they could do—they were meant to make Jewish people feel like they didn't belong, like they weren't even human.

THE NAZIS CONTROLLED EVERYTHING. They decided who could work, who could go to school, and even who could walk down certain streets. At first, Jewish families were banned from public places like parks, swimming pools, and libraries. That meant no more afternoons reading in the library or playing in the park with friends. But the restrictions didn't stop there. Jewish children were forced to leave their schools and attend separate Jewish-only schools. Teachers lost their jobs if they were Jewish. Doctors weren't allowed to treat non-Jewish patients.

Then came the yellow stars. Every Jewish person had to wear a yellow Star of David sewn onto their clothing at all times. It was meant to mark them, to make them stand out in a crowd. It wasn't just a piece of fabric—it was a symbol that told the world they were different, and under Nazi rule, different meant unwelcome. Some people in Amsterdam still treated Jewish neighbors with kindness, but others began looking away or avoiding them completely.

Even though the Franks had been in the Netherlands for years, Otto and Edith knew they were running out of time. They had heard about what was happening to Jewish people in Germany and other parts of Europe. Families were being taken from their homes and sent to work camps. At first, no one knew much about these camps, but people who had managed to escape told stories of terrible conditions, forced labor, and brutal treatment.

Then, the arrests started in Amsterdam. At night, Nazi officers would come knocking on doors, dragging families from their homes. Some people were taken from the streets in broad daylight. Others were betrayed by neighbors looking for a reward. Jewish families began disappearing, and no one knew where they were being sent.

The Nazis called it "deportation," as if people were simply being moved somewhere else, but there were too many whispers, too many unanswered questions. Trains were seen leaving Amsterdam, packed with Jewish men, women, and children. Those who were taken never returned. The fear spread through the Jewish community, and many realized they had two choices—wait to be taken or find a way to hide.

. . .

For Otto Frank, the decision had already been made. He had spent months preparing a secret space in his office building, slowly gathering supplies and making arrangements with trusted friends. When Margot received her deportation notice in July 1942, he knew they couldn't wait any longer. The Franks disappeared from their home and entered the Secret Annex, knowing they might never be able to return.

Living in hiding was the only way to stay safe, but it came with enormous risks. The Nazis had made it illegal to help Jewish families hide, which meant that anyone caught helping them could be arrested or even killed. Even trusted friends had to be extremely careful when bringing food, supplies, and news from the outside world. A single mistake—a misplaced word, a suspicious delivery, a sound heard through the walls—could mean discovery.

Otto Frank's plan to hide to keep his family safe

Otto Frank had seen the warning signs long before most people realized how dangerous life was becoming. He had already moved his family once, leaving Germany when it became clear that Jewish people were no longer safe there. He had hoped the Netherlands would be different, but now the same threats had followed them to Amsterdam. New laws were passed every week, each one taking away another right. Businesses were seized, schools were segregated, and Jewish families were being forced out of their homes. Deportations had started, and no one knew exactly where people were being taken. The one thing Otto did know was that none of them were coming back.

HE UNDERSTOOD what had to be done. If his family stayed in their home, it was only a matter of time before they would be arrested and sent away like so many others. The only way to survive was to disappear. The problem was, finding a safe hiding place wasn't easy. It had to be somewhere secret, somewhere no one would think to look. It had to be close enough to people they trusted, so they could get food and supplies. And most importantly, it had to be a place where they could stay for a long time, because once they went into hiding, there would be no leaving.

. . .

For months, Otto worked on a plan without telling his daughters, Anne and Margot. He didn't want them to worry, and there was always the risk that if they knew too much, they might say something by accident. Only a few trusted friends were involved, people he had known for years and knew he could count on. One of them was Miep Gies, an employee in his company, who, along with her husband Jan and a few others, would play a major role in keeping them safe.

The hiding place was inside Otto's own business, in a section of the building that wasn't easily visible from the street. Behind a bookcase on the upper floors was a secret set of rooms, which became known as the Secret Annex. It wasn't large, but it had enough space for Otto, Edith, Margot, and Anne. Another family, the Van Pels, would also be hiding with them, along with a man named Fritz Pfeffer.

Setting up the Annex was a slow and careful process. Otto had to be cautious, gathering supplies little by little so that no one would become suspicious. Furniture was moved in quietly, canned food was stored away, and thick curtains were added to the windows. The entrance was hidden behind a bookshelf, which looked like it was just part of the office.

EVERY DETAIL HAD to be planned. They would have to stay completely silent during the day when people were working in the offices below. They couldn't run water, walk too loudly, or even flush the toilet at certain times. At night, when the building was empty, they would have more freedom to move around, but the danger was always there. If anyone heard them, if anything seemed unusual, it could lead to their discovery.

OTTO ALSO HAD to think about what his family would need, not just to survive, but to live. He made sure to bring books, notebooks, and anything that would help them stay busy. He knew that hiding would be mentally and emotionally difficult, especially for Anne, who was used to being active and surrounded by friends.

. . .

THE PLAN WAS IN PLACE, but the Franks didn't move in right away. Otto hoped they might have more time. But when Margot received a letter ordering her to report for work duty in July 1942, he knew there was no more waiting. It was happening faster than they had expected. If Margot reported to the authorities, she would be sent away. If she refused, the whole family would be in danger.

Moving into the Secret Annex

The Secret Annex was never meant to be a home. It was a hidden space, a last resort for survival. When the Frank family stepped inside on July 6, 1942, they were leaving behind everything familiar—their home, their neighborhood, and any sense of normal life. They had planned for this, but nothing could truly prepare them for what it would mean to live in hiding.

The space itself was small and cramped. It was located in the back of Otto Frank's business building, hidden behind a moveable bookcase. From the outside, no one would have guessed that people were living there. Inside, there were a few small rooms, narrow hallways, and steep stairs that led to an attic. The Franks had the lower section of the

Annex, while the upper area would soon be shared with another family—the Van Pels.

The Van Pels family joined them a week later. Hermann and Auguste Van Pels had been friends of Otto's through business, and like the Franks, they knew that staying in their own home was no longer safe. Their son, Peter, was sixteen—three years older than Anne. That brought the number of people in the Annex to seven.

A few months later, an eighth person arrived. Fritz Pfeffer, a dentist and a family friend, was also looking for a place to hide. Otto agreed to take him in, though it meant even less space for everyone. Anne had to share her small room with him, something she was not happy about. She was used to having her own space, and Pfeffer's quiet, serious personality clashed with her energy and strong opinions.

With so many people living in such a small area, life in the Annex quickly became a test of patience. Every sound had to be kept to a minimum. During the day, when workers were in the offices below, no one could speak above a whisper. They had to walk carefully, avoiding any loud footsteps. Running water and flushing the toilet had to wait until the building was empty. If they made too much noise, someone might hear and alert the authorities.

There was no fresh air, no sunshine, no stepping outside. The windows were covered with thick curtains to keep anyone from seeing inside. Food was limited, brought in by their trusted helpers, but rationing meant that meals were often small and repetitive. The days stretched on, and the reality of their situation settled in.

Despite the fear and tension, they did their best to create some kind of routine. Otto encouraged the children to continue studying. Margot and Anne read books, practiced their writing, and tried to keep up with schoolwork. The adults found small ways to stay busy—cooking, cleaning, and listening to the radio for news about the war.

Sharing a space with seven other people wasn't easy. Personalities clashed, tempers flared, and small disagreements became bigger arguments. Anne, who had always been outspoken, found it especially difficult. She struggled with feeling trapped and misunderstood. Her diary became her escape, a place where she could express everything she was thinking and feeling.

Each person in the Annex handled their situation differently. Otto remained calm, trying to keep the peace. Edith worried constantly about the future. Margot stayed quiet, avoiding conflict. Peter kept to himself, not sure how to handle Anne's strong personality. The Van Pels often argued, especially Hermann and Auguste, who didn't always agree on how to handle their situation. Fritz Pfeffer, used to living alone, found it difficult to adjust to life with so many people around him.

What life was like in hiding

Life in the Secret Annex followed strict routines. Every day was planned carefully because even the smallest mistake could put everyone in danger. The eight people living in the small space had to adjust to new rules, new habits, and new challenges that they had never faced before.

Mornings started early. By 6:00 AM, everyone was awake, quietly getting dressed and preparing for the long day ahead. They had to move carefully, making as little noise as possible. The building below was a functioning business, and the workers arrived at 8:30 AM. That meant that by then, the Annex had to fall completely silent.

Breakfast was eaten quickly, often consisting of stale bread, margarine, or oatmeal, depending on what their helpers were able to bring them. Water had to be used sparingly. The plumbing couldn't be used too much during the day because the sound of flushing toilets or running water could be heard downstairs.

From 8:30 AM to 12:30 PM, no one could speak above a whisper. There was no walking around unless absolutely necessary, and if anyone did move, it had to be done in socks to keep footsteps from making noise on the wooden floors. Books, newspapers, and letters were read silently. Writing was done carefully so that the scratch of a pencil wouldn't echo. If someone coughed or sneezed, they had to muffle the sound as much as possible. Any noise could mean discovery.

At 12:30 PM, there was a brief moment of relief. The office workers left for lunch, and for about half an hour, the Annex was free to make some noise. The toilet could be flushed, people could stretch their legs, and food could be prepared. This was the time when they ate their biggest meal of the day, which usually wasn't much—potatoes, beans, or whatever their helpers had managed to bring.

By 1:00 PM, silence returned. The workers came back downstairs, and the Annex became still once again. Afternoons were long and difficult. Without being able to move freely, time seemed to slow down. Margot and Anne spent much of this time studying, reading, or writing. Anne wrote in her diary often, recording her thoughts and frustrations about life in hiding. She wrote about the arguments between people in the Annex, her feelings about each person, and her dreams for the future.

The adults kept themselves occupied as best they could. Otto read books and helped the children with their studies. Edith and Auguste prepared food, though there wasn't much to cook. Hermann Van Pels often worried about their situation, while Fritz Pfeffer, the dentist, tried to keep to himself when he wasn't arguing with Anne over their shared space.

The tension of being stuck in such a small space never went away. With eight people living together, there were frequent disagreements. Anne and her mother didn't always get along, and she often felt that her sister, Margot, was treated better. She found Fritz Pfeffer annoying and often complained about him in her diary. The Van Pels had their own struggles, with Hermann and Auguste arguing often, especially about food.

Food was one of the biggest challenges. Because they couldn't go outside, they depended entirely on their helpers to bring them supplies. Rations were small, and there were times when there wasn't enough. Some days, they had to eat the same meal over and over again. Bread became hard, potatoes rotted, and fresh vegetables were rare. Hunger became a constant feeling.

Nighttime brought both relief and fear. Once the office workers left for the day, the people in the Annex could finally move around more freely. They could whisper instead of mouthing words, stretch their legs, and go about small tasks without the fear of being overheard. But nighttime also brought danger. Any sound from outside—a creaking floorboard, a car stopping in the street, unfamiliar voices—could mean that someone was coming for them.

The air raids were another source of fear. At night, the sound of bombs dropping and sirens blaring filled the streets of Amsterdam. The war was raging on, and even though they couldn't see it, they could hear it all around them.

4

ANNE'S DIARY

Writing had always been a part of Anne Frank's life. Long before she ever went into hiding, she filled notebooks with stories, letters, and observations about the world around her. She didn't just write for school assignments—she wrote because she loved it. It was a way for her to express her thoughts, share her feelings, and make sense of everything happening in her life.

Words came easily to her. She was always full of opinions, always ready to tell a story or describe something in detail. If something upset her, she wrote about it. If something made her happy, she wrote about that too. Even when she wasn't putting words on paper, she was talking, thinking, and figuring out how she wanted to say things.

On June 12, 1942, Anne turned thirteen. It was a birthday like any other, filled with small gifts, sweet treats, and the warmth of family. One of the presents she received that day would change the way her story would be remembered forever—a red-and-white checkered diary.

She had seen it in a shop window days before and had been hoping she would get it. The moment she unwrapped it, she knew exactly what she wanted to do with it. She would write in it every day, filling its pages with her thoughts, dreams, and everything that mattered to her.

This diary wasn't just a place to write—it was a friend. She even gave it a name: Kitty. Instead of writing "Dear Diary" at the beginning of her entries, she wrote to Kitty as if it were a person. That made it feel more personal, more like a conversation than just words on a page.

She wrote about school, her friendships, her family, and the things she noticed about the world. She wrote honestly, never holding back how she felt. If she was frustrated, she let it out. If she was excited, her words showed it.

Only a few weeks after receiving the diary, everything changed. Her family went into hiding, leaving their home and stepping into the small, hidden world of the Secret Annex. The diary became even more important after that. There were no more friends to talk to, no more afternoons spent playing outside. She couldn't go to school, couldn't visit neighbors, couldn't live the way she had before. But she could still write.

Writing gave her something to focus on. It was her way of staying connected to the outside world, even though she couldn't be part of it anymore. She wrote about the Annex, about the people living in it, about how she felt being trapped in such a small space. Some days, she wrote about hope—about what she wanted to do after the war, about her dreams of becoming a writer or a journalist. Other days, she wrote about frustration—about the endless waiting, the arguments between the people in the Annex, and the fear of being discovered.

No one else in the Annex saw the diary the way she did. To them, it was just a notebook. To Anne, it was something more. It was the one place where she could be completely honest. There was no need to hold anything back, no need to pretend.

Over time, her writing became stronger, more thoughtful. She wasn't just recording events—she was trying to understand them. She thought about human nature, about fairness, about the way the world worked. She wrote about feeling lonely even though she was surrounded by people.

How her diary became her best friend

The walls of the Annex kept her hidden from the outside world, but they also separated her from the life she once knew. There were no more school days spent chatting with friends, no afternoons riding bikes through the city, no birthday parties or sleepovers. Even though she was living with seven other people, there were times when she felt completely alone.

That was when her diary became more than just a notebook. It became her best friend.

She named it Kitty, as if it were a real person. Writing to "Kitty" made it feel like she was having a conversation rather than just writing down events. She could tell Kitty anything—her fears, her frustrations, her hopes for the future. She didn't have to hold anything back. Unlike the people in the Annex,

Kitty never interrupted, never argued, never judged her.

Anne had always been opinionated, and life in hiding didn't change that. She had strong thoughts about everything—the people she lived with, the way adults treated her, the war, and even herself. She wrote about the tensions in the Annex, the small annoyances that came from being stuck in such a small space. She wrote about her mother and how she often felt misunderstood. She wrote about Margot, her older sister, and how different they were.

There were moments when she felt hopeful, and Kitty was the first to hear about them. She dreamed about what life would be like after the war. She imagined going back to school, traveling the world, becoming a writer. But there were also moments when fear crept in, when she wondered if she would ever get to do those things. Kitty became the place where she worked through those emotions.

Writing helped her understand herself. As time passed, her diary entries became deeper, more thoughtful. She wasn't just recording what happened each day—she was trying to make sense of the world. She wrote about the way people treated each other, about injustice, about why some people had power while others didn't.

Kitty became the one constant in a life that felt uncertain. The war outside was unpredictable, the future was unknown, and every day in the Annex brought new challenges. But no matter what happened, Anne could always pick up her diary and write.

What Anne wrote about

Some days, she wrote about the little things—what food they had to eat, what books she was reading, how bored she felt being stuck inside. Other days, she wrote about the bigger things—the war, the fear of being discovered, the feeling of being trapped. There were days when she was hopeful, imagining what she would do when she could finally leave the Secret Annex. Then there were days when everything felt overwhelming, when the uncertainty of the future seemed too much to bear.

She wrote about the people around her, describing each of them in detail. She wrote about her father, Otto, who she admired and trusted more than anyone. She wrote about her mother, Edith, and how they struggled to understand each other.

She wrote about Margot, her older sister, who was quiet and studious, the complete opposite of Anne's loud and opinionated personality.

She also wrote about the Van Pels family and Fritz Pfeffer, the others hiding with them. She noticed their habits, their tempers, and their quirks. Sometimes, she wrote about how much they annoyed her—the arguments, the tension, the way it felt like there was no space to breathe. Other times, she wrote with understanding, realizing that everyone in the Annex was scared, just like she was.

Her thoughts weren't always about life in hiding. She thought a lot about herself—who she was, what kind of person she wanted to be. She questioned her own feelings, wondering why she sometimes felt lonely even when she was surrounded by people. She wrote about wanting to be treated like an adult, about wanting to be taken seriously.

She also wrote about love. In the Annex, she found herself drawn to Peter Van Pels. At first, she didn't think much of him, but over time, she started to see him differently. She wrote about their conversations, about how he was one of the few people she could talk to when she felt overwhelmed. She wondered if what she was feeling was love or just a need for comfort.

Her dreams for the future were some of the most powerful things she wrote about. She didn't want to just grow up and live an ordinary life. She wanted to be a writer. She wanted to travel. She wanted to do something important. Even while living in the Annex, with no way of knowing what the future held, she still held onto that dream.

The hardships of hiding

Life in the Secret Annex was filled with challenges that never went away. The space was small, and with eight people living together, there was no such thing as privacy. The days felt endless, each one blending into the next. The silence during working hours made it difficult to do anything without feeling trapped, and the fear of being discovered never disappeared.

Anne wrote about all of it in her diary. She wrote about the hunger, which became worse as the war dragged on. Food was scarce, and what little they had wasn't always fresh. Bread went stale, vegetables spoiled, and sometimes meals consisted of little more than watery soup. There were times when there wasn't enough to go around, and rationing became a daily struggle. Arguments about food happened more often than anyone wanted to admit.

She wrote about the cold in the winter. The Annex had no heating, and blankets could only do so much. The floors were freezing, and the air felt sharp. Layers of clothing helped, but there was no escaping the chill. Summer brought its own problems. The heat inside the Annex became unbearable, and opening windows wasn't an option.

She wrote about the tension that filled the air. There was no way to avoid disagreements when everyone was crammed into the same small space day after day. The Van Pels family argued often, and Anne found herself frustrated with the adults. Everyone had different ideas about how things should be done, and those differences led to sharp words and long silences.

Fear was always present. Any noise outside the Annex could mean discovery. If someone knocked on the building door too loudly, if voices were heard in the alley, if a dog barked for too long, hearts pounded and breath was held. At night, the sound of bombings and sirens reminded them that war was not just a distant idea—it was all around them.

But there were also moments that made hiding a little more bearable. Anne held onto those moments and recorded them in her diary. Laughter still found its way into the Annex. Sometimes it came from a joke shared between Peter and Anne, or from a mistake someone made while cooking. Other times, it was caused by the ridiculousness of their situation—how a squeaky floorboard could send everyone into panic, or how they had to whisper even when they wanted to argue.

5

DISCOVERY AND CAPTURE

The longer the Franks and the others stayed in the Secret Annex, the more exhausting life became. Every single day was filled with rules and routines that could never be broken. Every step had to be careful, every sound had to be muffled, and every movement had to be controlled. The fear never left.

For over two years, the people in hiding lived with the constant tension of not knowing what would happen next. Some days were calm, but the worry was always in the back of their minds. The smallest noise could be a reason to panic. A creak in the floorboards, the sound of footsteps outside, or the sudden ringing of the office phone downstairs could send a wave of terror through the Annex.

The war outside wasn't slowing down. Air raids became more frequent, and explosions rattled the windows at night. News from the radio told of battles, bombings, and more Jewish families being taken away. The world was changing, but for the eight people in the Annex, time felt frozen.

The tension inside wasn't just from fear of discovery—it was from being stuck in the same small space with the same people for more than two years. No one had privacy, and every little habit, every small annoyance, built up over time. Arguments happened more often. Anne wrote in her diary about the fights between the Van Pels family, about the disagreements between the adults, and about how hard it was to always be quiet and obedient.

Food shortages made things even worse. As the war went on, it became harder for their helpers to bring supplies. Meals became smaller, and hunger became a daily struggle. Sometimes, they had to eat the same thing for days in a row. The frustration of being trapped, combined with the stress of survival, made every emotion feel stronger.

Anne kept writing. It was the only thing that gave her a sense of freedom. She poured her emotions into her diary—her anger, her hopes, her sadness, and her dreams for the future. She tried to stay positive, but there were days when the fear felt overwhelming.

Every knock at the door, every unfamiliar sound, was a reminder that they could be discovered at any moment. The Nazis had already arrested so many people. Even though they had been safe for two years, they knew their luck could run out. It was only a matter of time.

The betrayal

No one knows for certain how the Annex was discovered. The Nazis had spies, informers, and a network of people who were willing to turn in Jewish families for rewards. Some believe that someone betrayed them—perhaps a worker in the building or a neighbor who had grown suspicious. Others think it may have been an accidental discovery. The only thing that is certain is that the safety they had held onto for so long was shattered that day.

That morning started like any other. The office workers had arrived below, and the people in the Annex were following their usual routine—silent, careful, waiting for the midday break when they could move more freely.

Then came the sound they had feared for so long. Loud footsteps on the stairs. A knock at the door. Voices that were unfamiliar. The sound of orders being given.

There was no time to escape. The Secret Annex was designed to keep people hidden, not to let them flee. The moveable bookcase was pushed aside, revealing the entrance to their hiding place. The people inside had nowhere to go. The fear they had lived with for two years had finally become real.

Armed officers from the Nazi police force entered the Annex. They searched the rooms, ordering everyone to gather their things. The Franks, the Van Pels, and Fritz Pfeffer were told they had five minutes to pack a bag. There was no time to think, no time to plan.

Anne's diary was left behind. Papers were scattered across the floor. The place that had once been their only refuge was now just another space controlled by the Nazis.

Anne and her family being arrested

Armed officers led them down the stairs, past the offices where people worked every day, unaware that eight people had been hiding just above them for two years. The Franks, the Van Pels, and Fritz Pfeffer were marched through the streets of Amsterdam. The city they had once called home was now a place of danger. People on the street may have recognized them, but no one spoke up, no one intervened. By then, everyone knew what happened to Jewish families when they were arrested.

They were taken to the headquarters of the Nazi police. The officers who had found them searched their bags, their pockets, taking anything of value. They were questioned, though there was little they could say that would change their fate. Their names were added to the long lists of Jewish people already taken before them.

That same day, they were sent to Westerbork, a transit camp in the Netherlands. The journey there was by truck, moving them like prisoners. When they arrived, they saw the endless rows of barracks, the barbed wire fences, the thousands of others who had been arrested before them. Westerbork was not the final destination—everyone there was waiting for the trains that would take them further, deeper into Nazi-controlled territory.

In the Annex, they had been careful, they had been cautious. For more than two years, they had followed every rule to avoid being caught. Now, none of it mattered. They had lost their freedom. They had lost their home. The fear they had lived with every day had become real.

There was no way to know what would happen next, but they all knew one thing: no one came back from where they were going.

6

THE JOURNEY TO THE CAMPS

The Franks, the Van Pels, and Fritz Pfeffer were no longer hiding. They were prisoners now, forced into a system designed to erase them. After their arrest, they were transported to Westerbork, a transit camp in the Netherlands. It was the first stop on a journey they could not control, a journey that would take them further from everything they had known.

Westerbork was not a place where people stayed for long. It was a camp where Jewish prisoners were held until the Nazis decided where to send them next. Thousands of people were crammed into long, wooden barracks with hardly any space to move. There were no real comforts, just rows of bunk beds, harsh rules, and endless waiting.

The Franks had spent two years in the Secret Annex, where silence was necessary for survival. Westerbork was different. The camp was noisy, filled with the sounds of footsteps, voices, orders being shouted. There was no place to be alone, no place to escape the reality of what was happening.

Everyone in the camp knew what the trains meant. Every week, hundreds of people were put onto cattle cars and taken east. No one knew exactly where they were going, but they had heard the rumors. They knew that once someone boarded a train, they rarely came back.

On September 3, 1944, it was their turn. Their names were on the list. The waiting was over. They were going to be sent away.

The train that carried them out of Westerbork was not made for people. It was a freight train, the kind used to transport goods, not passengers. There were no seats, no windows, no space to sit or lie down. The doors were locked from the outside. The journey lasted for days, with no food, no water, no way to escape.

There was no telling where they were going, only that the train never stopped for long. When it finally slowed, the doors were thrown open, and the truth was revealed. They had arrived at Auschwitz.

Everything changed the moment they stepped off the train. Guards shouted orders. Families were separated. Men in one direction, women in another. Luggage was taken, belongings stolen, names replaced with numbers.

The Franks had been together for so long, but now, they were torn apart. Otto was sent to the men's section. Edith, Margot, and Anne were sent with the women. The Van Pels were divided, and Fritz Pfeffer was taken away.

Life in the concentration camps

The moment Anne and her family stepped off the train at Auschwitz, everything about their lives changed. The world they had known—the Secret Annex, the city of Amsterdam, even the crowded barracks of Westerbork—was gone. This was something else entirely. The camp was surrounded by tall fences topped with barbed wire, patrolled by guards with weapons. Towering chimneys filled the sky with thick, dark smoke.

THE PRISONERS WERE FORCED into lines, divided immediately. Men to one side, women to another.

Otto was separated from Edith, Margot, and Anne. That was the last time Anne ever saw her father.

Everything they carried was taken from them. The little they had left—clothes, shoes, anything in their hands—was no longer theirs. Guards shouted orders, pushing them forward. They were herded into a large building where they were stripped of their clothes, their hair was shaved, and a number was tattooed on their arms. Their names no longer mattered. They were now just numbers in a system that had no mercy.

The conditions inside Auschwitz were unlike anything they had ever experienced. The barracks were overcrowded, filled with people packed so tightly there was hardly enough space to lie down. The wooden bunks had no mattresses, only straw or thin blankets, and the cold air seeped through the walls. There was no privacy, no comfort.

Food was scarce, barely enough to survive. Watery soup, a small piece of bread, maybe a little bit of potato—this was all they received each day. Hunger was constant. People grew weaker with each passing day, their bodies shrinking, their strength disappearing.

THE DAYS WERE long and brutal. Prisoners were forced to work from morning until night, regardless of how sick or weak they were. Some were sent to labor outside in freezing temperatures, others to factories or dangerous tasks inside the camp. Anyone who could not keep up was punished.

FEAR WAS EVERYWHERE. Punishments were harsh, and guards showed no kindness. People who fell behind were beaten. Those who were too weak to work were taken away, never to be seen again. The chimneys in the distance told everyone where they had gone.

ANNE WAS ONLY FIFTEEN, but she was no longer treated as a child. In Auschwitz, no one was spared from suffering. She had always been full of energy, always ready to talk and share her thoughts. Now, survival took all of her strength.

Despite everything, she had her mother and sister. Edith did everything she could to take care of Anne and Margot, even when she had nothing to give. They shared every bit of food they could, offering comfort in a place where kindness was rare.

Winter arrived, and the cold became unbearable. There were no warm clothes, only thin uniforms that did nothing to keep out the freezing air. Many prisoners didn't survive the brutal temperatures. Illness spread quickly, and there was no medicine, no treatment, no rest for those who fell sick.

Anne and Margot being sent to Bergen-Belsen

By the fall of 1944, Auschwitz was changing. The war was turning against Germany, and the Nazis were trying to cover up their crimes. Trains carried prisoners away, moving them to other camps as the Soviet army got closer. Among those selected for transport were Anne and Margot Frank.

They had already endured months of starvation, hard labor, and sickness. Their bodies had grown weak, but they were still considered young enough to work. Edith Frank was not chosen to go with them. She was left behind at Auschwitz, separated from her daughters just as Otto had been months earlier.

The journey from Auschwitz to Bergen-Belsen was another brutal trip in a crowded train car. There was no food, no water, and no place to sit. People were packed so tightly that there was barely room to breathe. Some didn't survive the journey. The ones who did arrived to find another nightmare waiting for them.

Bergen-Belsen was not a work camp like Auschwitz. It was a place where people were sent when they were no longer needed for labor. There were no gas chambers there, but that didn't mean survival was any easier. The conditions were horrifying. Disease spread rapidly, food was nearly nonexistent, and prisoners were left to die slowly from starvation and sickness.

Anne and Margot had only each other now. They had lost everything—their home, their parents, their friends. Bergen-Belsen was overcrowded, filled with people who had been taken from other camps.

There were no proper barracks, just ragged tents and makeshift shelters. The winter was harsh, and they had no warm clothing to protect them from the freezing temperatures.

Food was even scarcer than at Auschwitz. A crust of bread or a thin, cold soup was all they had. People fought over scraps. Many were too weak to move, collapsing where they stood. The camp was filled with death. Bodies were left unburied, sickness spread everywhere, and hope was nearly impossible to hold onto.

Anne had always been strong-willed. She had survived years of hiding, had written about her dreams of becoming a writer, had found hope even in the darkness of the Annex. But Bergen-Belsen broke even the strongest spirits. She and Margot became weaker with each passing day. They had been fighting to survive for too long, and their bodies could no longer keep up.

By early 1945, typhus had spread through the camp. Margot, once healthy and studious, was so weak that she could no longer stand. She died first, unable to fight the disease any longer. Not long after, Anne followed.

Their journey had taken them from a loving home in Amsterdam to the cramped space of the

Secret Annex, to the horrors of Auschwitz, and finally to Bergen-Belsen. They had survived longer than many others, but in the end, the war took them too.

When the camp was liberated just weeks later, it was too late for Anne and Margot. They had been so close to seeing the end of the war, but the suffering they had endured had already taken everything from them.

7

ANNE'S LEGACY

When the war ended in 1945, Otto Frank was alone. He had survived Auschwitz, but his wife and daughters had not. He didn't know what had happened to them at first. Like so many others, he searched for names on lists, asked people who had been in the camps, and waited for news.

Slowly, the truth reached him. Edith had died in Auschwitz in January 1945. Anne and Margot had been sent to Bergen-Belsen and died there in early 1945, just weeks before the camp was liberated. The daughters he had protected for so long, the ones he had carried into hiding, were gone.

He had lost his entire family. The life he had built in Amsterdam was no longer there. The Annex was empty. The world had moved forward, but he was left with memories and grief.

Then he returned to the place where he had last been with them. The Secret Annex, hidden behind the bookcase, was still there. The rooms were silent, but the walls held reminders of the people who had once lived there in fear and hope.

Miep Gies, one of the friends who had helped the Franks hide, had kept something for him. After the family was arrested, she had gone into the Annex and found Anne's diary. She had gathered the scattered pages, the notebooks filled with Anne's words, and had kept them safe. She had hoped to return them to Anne one day. Now, she placed them in Otto's hands.

At first, Otto couldn't bring himself to read it. It was too painful. But as he slowly made his way through the pages, he saw his daughter again—not just the girl who had lived in hiding, but the young writer she had become. She had written everything—her thoughts, her frustrations, her dreams, her fears. She had hoped for a future. She had wanted to be a writer.

Her words had survived, even though she had not.

He made a decision. The world needed to read

what Anne had written. Her diary wasn't just a record of her time in hiding—it was a voice that had been taken too soon. He shared it with publishers, and in 1947, it was printed as *The Diary of Anne Frank.*

People read it. They connected with Anne's words. They saw the war through her eyes, felt her hopes and struggles, and understood what had been lost. Her diary was translated into dozens of languages. It was read in schools, studied in classrooms, turned into plays and films.

Otto spent the rest of his life sharing her story. He answered letters from people around the world who had been moved by Anne's words. He spoke about what had happened, not just to his family, but to the millions of others who had suffered.

How Anne's words were published

When Otto Frank first held Anne's diary in his hands, it was almost too painful to read. Every word on the page brought her back—the way she wrote, the way she saw the world, the way she had believed in a future she never got to see. It was as if she was speaking to him again.

Page by page, he read the life she had recorded in the Secret Annex. The way she described their days in hiding, the frustrations of sharing a small space, the hope she held onto despite everything. She had written about her family, her dreams of becoming a writer, and her thoughts on the world around her. She had captured the fear, the waiting, and the reality of what it meant to be Jewish during the war.

As difficult as it was to go through her words, Otto knew they needed to be shared. Anne had wanted to publish her diary one day—she had even started rewriting parts of it to make it better. She had believed that her story was important. Otto decided that if she could not do it herself, he would do it for her.

At first, it wasn't easy to find a publisher. The war had only just ended, and people were still trying to make sense of everything that had happened. But Otto didn't give up. He shared the diary with historians and friends, and soon, people began to realize how powerful Anne's words were.

In 1947, her diary was published for the first time in Dutch under the title *Het Achterhuis*, which means *The Secret Annex*. It was not just another book about the war—it was a deeply personal story told through the eyes of a young girl who had lived through it. Readers were drawn to Anne's voice. She wasn't just listing facts or writing about battles; she was sharing her thoughts, her feelings, and her dreams.

Word spread quickly. People outside the Netherlands wanted to read it too, and within a few years, the diary was translated into other languages. By the 1950s, it had been published in German, French, and English. In English, it was titled *The Diary of a Young Girl*.

More and more people read her words, and the diary became more than just a book—it became a symbol. Schools began using it to teach students about the Holocaust. Readers connected with Anne because she wasn't just a victim of history; she was a teenager with hopes and struggles, just like them.

In 1955, Anne's story was turned into a play, and in 1959, a film adaptation was released. Her words reached people in new ways, bringing her experiences to audiences who might never have picked up the book.

Over the years, the diary continued to spread. It was translated into more than 70 languages and became one of the most widely read books in history. Millions of people, young and old, found themselves moved by Anne's words.

Otto Frank dedicated the rest of his life to sharing his daughter's story. He traveled, spoke about what had happened, and worked to make sure the lessons of the Holocaust were never forgotten. He helped turn the Secret Annex into a museum, where visitors could walk through the same rooms where Anne had once written in her diary.

Anne had dreamed of becoming a writer. She had hoped that her words would matter. In the end, they did. Her diary became one of the most important books of all time—not just because of what happened to her, but because of the way she wrote, the way she made people feel, and the way she reminded the world of what should never happen again.

How Anne's diary has inspired millions of people around the world

Anne Frank never lived to see how much her words would mean to the world. When she wrote in her diary, she wasn't thinking about becoming famous. She was writing for herself, for Kitty, her imaginary friend. She was writing because she needed a way to express everything she was feeling while she was trapped in hiding. But after her diary was published, it became more than just the personal thoughts of a young girl—it became a voice for millions.

Her words have been read by people all over the world. Children, teenagers, and adults from different countries, different backgrounds, and different generations have connected with Anne's story. Her diary has been used in schools to teach history, to help people understand what happened during the Holocaust, and to show how discrimination and hatred can destroy lives.

One of the reasons her diary has touched so many people is because of how honest she was. She didn't just write about the war—she wrote about herself. She wrote about feeling misunderstood, about wanting to be independent, about struggling with her emotions. She wrote about her dreams of becoming a writer, about the kind of person she wanted to be. She wrote about hope, even when the world around her was full of fear.

Her words have inspired people in many ways. Some have been moved by her courage, by the way she continued to believe in the goodness of people even when she was living in fear. Others have been inspired by her determination to write, to put her thoughts on paper even when she had no idea if anyone would ever read them.

Over the years, people have written letters to Otto Frank, telling him how much Anne's diary meant to them. Many readers have felt as if they knew Anne, as if she were a friend who had shared her deepest thoughts with them. Her words made history feel personal. She was not just a name in a textbook—she was a real girl with real feelings, and that has helped people understand the past in a way that numbers and dates never could.

Her story has also led to important discussions about tolerance and human rights. People have used her diary to talk about the dangers of discrimination, about the importance of standing up against injustice. Her words have encouraged people to be kinder, to treat others with respect, and to make sure that what happened to her never happens again.

The Anne Frank House in Amsterdam, the place where she hid for two years, has become a museum visited by millions. People from all over the world walk through the small rooms of the Secret Annex, seeing where she lived, where she wrote, and where she held onto hope. It is a place of remembrance, but also a place of learning.

Anne's words have lasted because they remind people of something important—that even in the darkest times, there is still light. That one voice, even one as young as hers, can make a difference. That stories matter, because they help us remember, they help us understand, and they help us do better.

She never got to grow up, never got to write the books she dreamed of writing. But through her diary, her words have reached more people than she ever could have imagined. And even though she didn't survive, her voice did.

CONCLUSION

Anne Frank's story is not just about the past. It's about the present and the future. Her words have lasted for decades, not because she was famous when she was alive, but because of what she left behind. She wrote about hope in a time of fear, about dreams in a place where there was no freedom. Her diary is a reminder of what happens when hatred goes unchecked, but it is also a reminder that even in the worst times, people still hold on to kindness, love, and hope.

Her diary has been read by millions, and yet, every person who reads it feels like they know her personally. That is part of why her story remains so powerful. She was just a girl. She argued with her mother. She had crushes. She wanted to be heard and understood. She had big dreams, just like any other teenager. The difference was that she lived during one of the darkest times in history, and that changed everything.

People continue to read her diary because it makes history feel real. It's easy to read about wars and think of them as something that happened long ago, something that doesn't connect to today. But Anne's words make it personal. She wasn't a soldier or a leader. She wasn't on a battlefield. She was just a girl hiding in an attic, trying to stay alive. That is why her story matters.

Her diary also teaches people about the dangers of discrimination. The Holocaust didn't happen overnight. It started with small things—laws that took away rights, schools that forced Jewish children out, businesses that were shut down. The more people ignored these things, the worse they got. Anne and her family went into hiding because the world around them had decided that Jewish people didn't belong. Her story is a reminder that standing up against injustice matters, because ignoring it only allows it to grow.

But her story isn't just about what was lost. It's also about resilience. She lived in fear, but she still wrote. She still believed in a future where things would be better. She still dreamed of being a writer, of traveling the world, of making a difference. Even when food was scarce, when silence was the only way to stay safe, when the war seemed endless, she still found ways to hold on to hope.

That is why people continue to visit the Anne Frank House. That is why her words are studied in schools, why people quote her when they talk about hope, why her diary is still being read all over the world. She didn't live to see her words published, but they became more powerful than she could have ever imagined.

Her story is still important today because the things she wrote about still matter. People still face discrimination. Wars still happen. Families still have to leave their homes because of violence. But Anne's diary reminds people that even when the world is cruel, people can choose to be kind. Even when things seem hopeless, there is still room for hope. Even when one voice is taken away, the words they leave behind can change the world.

She was just one person. One voice. One diary. But her story has lasted, because the lessons inside it are too important to forget.

APPENDIX

Timeline

1929: Anne is born

Anne Frank was born on June 12, 1929, in Frankfurt, Germany. She was the second daughter of Otto and Edith Frank. Her older sister, Margot, was born in 1926. At the time, Germany was going through difficult changes. The country had lost World War I, and many people were struggling. During Anne's early years, her family lived comfortably, but things in Germany were getting worse, especially for Jewish families like hers.

1933: The Frank family leaves Germany

When Anne was four years old, a man named Adolf Hitler became the leader of Germany. He and his followers, known as the Nazis, began making new laws that took away rights from Jewish people. Otto and Edith saw what was happening and decided it was no longer safe for their family to stay in Germany. Like many other Jewish families, they moved to another country to find safety. In 1933, they left Frankfurt and settled in Amsterdam, Netherlands.

1934–1939: A new life in the Netherlands

Anne adjusted to her new life in Amsterdam. She learned Dutch, made friends, and started school. Otto Frank started a business, and the family found a home in the city. Life in Amsterdam was peaceful compared to Germany, but across Europe, things were changing. The Nazis were gaining power, and tensions were rising.

In 1939, Germany invaded Poland, marking the beginning of World War II. Although the war had started, the Netherlands remained neutral at first, meaning they were not involved in the fighting. The Frank family hoped they had found a safe place, but things would soon take a turn for the worse.

1940: The Nazis invade the Netherlands

In May 1940, Germany invaded the Netherlands. It happened quickly, and soon the Nazis controlled the country. New laws were made that targeted

Jewish people, restricting where they could go and what they could do. Anne and Margot could no longer attend the same schools as their friends. Otto lost control of his business because Jewish people were not allowed to own companies. Life for Jewish families became more dangerous.

1942: Going into hiding

On Anne's 13th birthday, June 12, 1942, she received a diary as a gift. She began writing in it right away, describing her daily life, thoughts, and feelings.

Just weeks later, on July 6, 1942, the Frank family went into hiding. The Nazis had started arresting Jewish families and sending them to concentration camps. When Margot received a notice that she had to report to a Nazi labor camp, the family knew they had no time left.

They moved into a hidden part of Otto's business building, which they called the Secret Annex. They were soon joined by the Van Pels family and Fritz Pfeffer, making a total of eight people living in the small space. For the next two years, they remained hidden, relying on helpers who brought them food and supplies.

1942–1944: Life in the Secret Annex

Anne continued writing in her diary while in

hiding. She wrote about the difficulties of living in such a small space, her frustrations with the people around her, and her hopes for the future. She dreamed of becoming a writer and believed that one day, she would be able to share her story with the world.

She also wrote about the war and what she heard on the radio. The people in the Annex followed the news carefully, hoping for signs that the war would end soon.

August 4, 1944: Discovery and arrest

After more than two years in hiding, the Secret Annex was raided by the Nazi police. Someone—though it is still unclear who—betrayed the people in hiding by telling the Nazis about their location. The Franks, the Van Pels, and Fritz Pfeffer were arrested and taken from the Annex. Their helpers, including Miep Gies and Johannes Kleiman, were also arrested, though some were later released.

August–September 1944: Deportation to Auschwitz

The people from the Secret Annex were sent to Westerbork, a transit camp in the Netherlands. They stayed there for several weeks before being put on a train to Auschwitz, a concentration camp in Poland. The journey lasted days, with the prisoners packed tightly into cattle cars with no food, water, or space to move.

Upon arrival at Auschwitz, the men and women were separated. Otto was taken away from his wife and daughters. The conditions in the camp were brutal. Prisoners were forced to do hard labor, given almost no food, and faced extreme weather with little protection.

October 1944: Anne and Margot are sent to Bergen-Belsen

As the war continued, the Nazis moved many prisoners to different camps. Anne and Margot were taken from Auschwitz to Bergen-Belsen, a concentration camp in Germany. By then, both girls were weak and malnourished. Bergen-Belsen was overcrowded, and disease spread quickly.

Early 1945: Anne and Margot's deaths

During the harsh winter, a disease called typhus spread through Bergen-Belsen. Margot became sick first, and Anne soon after. With no medical care and barely any food, neither could recover. Margot died first, followed shortly by Anne.

Their exact dates of death are unknown, but it is believed they died in February or March 1945. Just weeks later, British soldiers arrived and liberated Bergen-Belsen. If Anne and Margot had survived just a little longer, they might have been saved.

1945: Otto Frank survives and returns to Amsterdam

Otto Frank was the only member of the Secret Annex to survive. He was freed when Auschwitz was liberated by Soviet soldiers in January 1945. After the war, he returned to Amsterdam, hoping to find his wife and daughters. When he learned that Anne and Margot had died, he was devastated.

Miep Gies, one of the family's helpers, had gone back to the Annex after the arrest and found Anne's diary. She had kept it safe, hoping to return it to Anne one day. When Otto came back, she gave it to him.

1947: Anne's diary is published

Otto read through Anne's diary and saw how much she had written about life in hiding. He knew how much she had wanted to be a writer. With the help of friends, he decided to share her story with the world. In 1947, *The Diary of a Young Girl* was published in Dutch.

Over the years, the diary was translated into dozens of languages and read by millions. Schools began using it to teach students about the Holocaust.

Anne's story became one of the most well-known accounts of life during World War II.

Facts About the Secret Annex

The Secret Annex was more than just a hiding place—it was a world of its own. For more than two years, eight people lived there, cut off from the outside world. Every day was a mix of fear, boredom, frustration, and hope. The space was small, the rules were strict, and survival depended on staying completely hidden.

The building where the Secret Annex was located was at 263 Prinsengracht in Amsterdam. It was the back section of Otto Frank's business, Opekta, which sold pectin for making jam. To the outside world, it was just another workplace. Behind a moveable bookcase, hidden from view, was the Annex where Anne and the others lived in silence, trying to escape Nazi persecution.

The Size of the Annex

It wasn't very big. The entire space was about 500 square feet—smaller than some apartments today. There were four small rooms, a tiny bathroom, and an attic. Eight people had to share that space without ever stepping outside.

Anne shared a room with Fritz Pfeffer, a dentist who was also in hiding. She didn't like sharing a room with an adult. He snored, took up too much space, and didn't always respect her need for quiet when she wanted to write. The Van Pels family—Hermann, Auguste, and their son Peter—lived in the largest room. Otto, Edith, and Margot Frank took another. The kitchen was also the living room, dining room, and the place where everyone gathered when it was safe to move around.

The Moveable Bookcase

One of the most famous parts of the Annex was the entrance. It wasn't just a regular door—it was hidden behind a bookcase. When Otto Frank and his helpers were preparing the space, they needed to make sure no one would find it. A swinging bookshelf was built to conceal the doorway. During the day, employees worked in the offices downstairs, never suspecting that eight people were hiding just a few feet away.

Life in Hiding

Every movement had to be controlled. During the workday, when people were in the offices below, no one in the Annex could speak above a whisper. They couldn't flush the toilet, run water, or even walk too loudly. The fear of being discovered was constant.

Once the workers left for the evening, life became a little more normal. People could talk, move around, and eat dinner together. But there was never a true sense of relaxation. There were still risks—unexpected visitors, deliveries, or noises that might draw attention to the hidden people above.

Anne wrote in her diary about how hard it was to live in such a small space with so many people. Tempers flared, arguments happened, and sometimes she felt trapped, not just physically but emotionally.

Food and Supplies

The people in the Annex depended entirely on their helpers—Miep Gies, Johannes Kleiman, Victor Kugler, and Bep Voskuijl—to bring them food, supplies, and news of the outside world. The helpers risked their own lives to keep them safe.

Food was often scarce. Rations during the war were limited, and finding enough to feed eight extra people was difficult. They ate a lot of beans and potatoes because they lasted a long time. Sometimes, they had to make do with whatever was available. Anne wrote about eating the same meals for weeks at a time.

Miep and the others also brought books, magazines, and paper for Anne to write on. Without them, life in the Annex would have been unbearable.

News from the Outside

The Annex had one connection to the outside world—a small radio. The people in hiding listened carefully to the news, hoping to hear signs that the war was turning in their favor. They learned about battles, air raids, and political changes. Every bit of news gave them hope that one day, they would be able to leave safely.

Anne followed world events closely. She wrote about them in her diary, thinking deeply about what was happening. She didn't just write about her daily life—she thought about the bigger picture, about justice, about what kind of world she wanted to live in after the war.

Celebrations in Hiding

Even in difficult times, the people in the Annex tried to hold on to traditions. They celebrated birthdays, including Anne's 14th and 15th while in hiding. The gifts were small—sometimes just a piece of fruit or a homemade card—but they still meant something.

They also celebrated Hanukkah and St. Nicholas

Day. Anne wrote about how they tried to make the holidays feel normal, even though there was no way to truly celebrate like they had before the war. It was a way to remind themselves that they were still a family, still people, even when the world outside saw them differently.

The Fear of Discovery

The Annex was not completely soundproof. People working in the warehouse below sometimes heard noises from upstairs. Once, a break-in happened downstairs, and the people in the Annex were terrified that the burglars might have discovered them. Any knock at the door or unfamiliar voice outside could mean the end of their safety.

Anne wrote about the fear they all felt when they heard unfamiliar sounds. There was always the possibility that someone would betray them. The more time passed, the more dangerous it became.

The Day It Ended

On August 4, 1944, the worst fear of the people in the Annex became a reality. Nazi police arrived and arrested everyone. To this day, no one knows for certain who betrayed them. Some believe it was a warehouse worker, while others think someone from the outside told the Nazis about the hiding place.

Their time in the Annex was over. After more

than two years of hiding, they were sent to concentration camps. Only Otto Frank survived.

What Remains Today

The Secret Annex is now part of the Anne Frank House, a museum dedicated to Anne's life and legacy. Visitors can walk through the small rooms, see the bookcase that once hid the entrance, and read quotes from Anne's diary on the walls.

Her story, and the story of the Annex, continues to be told. The space where she lived, wrote, and dreamed of the future is still there, a reminder of what happened and why remembering it matters.

Discussion Questions

What would it feel like to go into hiding?

Anne and her family had to leave behind everything—her home, her friends, her school, and her freedom. They couldn't go outside, couldn't speak loudly, and couldn't live like they used to. Thinking about this raises a lot of important questions. What would be the hardest part of living in hiding? How would someone pass the time in such a small space? What kinds of things would be missed the most?

Why do you think Anne kept writing in her diary?

Even when life in the Annex was difficult, Anne continued to write. She didn't just write about events—she wrote about her emotions, her thoughts, and her dreams. Why do people write about their feelings? How does writing help people deal with difficult situations? If Anne hadn't written her diary, would the world have ever known her story?

What does courage mean?

Anne showed courage in many ways, but she wasn't the only one. The people who hid her family risked their lives to help them. Otto Frank had to make tough choices to protect his family. The people in the Annex had to live with fear every day, yet they kept going. What does it mean to be brave? Is courage always about big actions, or can small choices be just as important?

Why do you think Anne believed people were good at heart?

Even after everything she had been through, Anne wrote that she still believed people were good at heart. That can be a hard idea to understand, especially knowing how unfairly Jewish people were treated during the war. Why would she feel that way? Do you think she still believed it later? What does it mean to hold onto hope even when things seem bad?

How can we stand up for others today?

Anne and her family had to go into hiding because of unfair laws. Many people ignored what was happening, but some people—like the helpers who brought food to the Annex—risked everything to help. How can people stand up for what's right today? Are there times when staying silent makes things worse? What are small ways to help others who are being treated unfairly?

What can we learn from Anne's words?

Anne wrote about kindness, courage, and hope. She dreamed of a future where she could be free. Even though she didn't survive, her words did. What do her words teach us about how to treat others? How do they help us understand the past? How can her story help create a better future?

www.ingramcontent.com/pod-product-compliance
Ingram Content Group UK Ltd.
Pitfield, Milton Keynes, MK11 3LW, UK
UKHW022302170225
455202UK00013B/674